The Village Show

Mum was in the garden pulling up onions.
Kate was helping her.
'Shall I pull some of these up?' she asked.
'Not on your life,' laughed Mum. 'Those are my
    prize beetroots.
    I'm entering them in the village show next week.'

There was a village show every year.
People grew flowers and vegetables or
  made cakes and jam and wine.
They entered them in the show and there
  were prizes for the best.

Dad was entering his elderberry wine.
'He won't win, though,' said Mum. 'Mrs
    Mudge's dandelion wine always wins.'
'Can I enter something?' asked Kate.
'Perhaps next year,' said Mum.

'I don't know why I can't enter something
    for the show,' said Kate to her sister.
    'Everybody else is going to.'
'Why don't we make something, too,' said Jo,
    'and keep it a secret?'

'That's a good idea,' said Kate. 'We could
    make some dandelion wine.'
'Why?' asked Jo.
'Because dandelion wine always wins,' said Kate.
    'We can ask Mrs Mudge how to make it.'

Mrs Mudge was working in her kitchen.
'Hello, Mrs Mudge,' said Kate. 'Will you tell us
  how you make your dandelion wine?'
'No I won't!' said Mrs Mudge. 'It's my secret.
  Why do you want to know?'

'I want to enter some in the show,' said Kate.
'I shouldn't bother,' laughed Mrs Mudge. 'My
   dandelion wine always wins first prize.'
'Somebody will beat you one of these days,' said
   Mr Mudge. 'And that will shake you.'

'I'm not going to give up,' said Kate to Jo.
   'Dandelion wine can't be that hard to make.'
'Shall we ask Mum?' asked Jo.
'No,' said Kate. 'It's our secret and I think
   we can manage on our own.'

The fields behind the cottages were
  covered in dandelions.
The girls picked lots and lots but
  it was very hard work.
Jo sighed. 'I hope you know what we're doing.'

They put all the flowers in a big pan.

'What goes in next?' asked Jo.

'Boiling water,' said Kate.

'You know we're not allowed that,' said Jo.

'I think cold is almost as good,' said Kate.

The girls filled the pan from the outside tap.
The mixture didn't look very exciting.
'How long do we have to wait?' asked Jo.
'It should be ready at the weekend,' said Kate,
  'but we have to put in other things.'

'Sugar is very important,' said Kate. 'I'll get
   my pocket money and we'll buy some.'
They went to the village shop.
'A bag of sugar, please,' said Kate, 'and
   a packet of wine gums.'

'How much sugar do we put in?' asked Jo.
'All of it,' said Kate, 'and all the wine gums.'
They tipped in the sugar and the wine gums and
  stirred the mixture with a stick.
'It's not doing much,' said Jo.

At the weekend, Kate thought the wine was ready.
'It has to be strained,' she said.
'What does strained mean?' asked Jo.
'It means we get all the dandelions out and
    just leave the liquid,' said Kate.

Kate put an old cloth over the bucket.
She poured the liquid through the cloth.
Then she threw the dandelion heads away.
'Is that it?' asked Jo. 'I thought
    it would be yellow.'

'I think it should be yellow,' said Kate.

   'Perhaps we should put something else in it.'

'I'll get my paints,' said Jo.

'We'll only use a little paint,' said Kate,

   'or we might spoil the wine.'

When the wine was yellow it was time
   to put it into bottles.
Kate borrowed three of Dad's.
'I think you should ask him,' said Jo.
'No,' said Kate. 'It's got to be a secret.'

'What about the corks?' asked Jo.

Kate didn't know what to do about the corks.

'We'll just have to ask Mrs Mudge,' she said.

The girls carried the bottles down to
    Mrs Mudge's cottage.

Mrs Mudge wasn't pleased to see the girls.
She was writing labels for her own dandelion wine.
'I'm not wasting good corks on silly
    games like that,' she said.
    'It takes years to learn how to make good wine.'

Mr Mudge was more helpful.

'I'll put some corks in for you,' he said.

Kate and Jo liked Mr Mudge.

They decided to let him in on the secret.

They told him how they had made the wine.

Mr Mudge shook with laughter.
'I don't think you'll beat Mrs Mudge,' he said.
   'She's very proud of her dandelion wine.'
'Well, we can try,' said Kate.
'You never know your luck,' laughed Mr Mudge.

'I'll put these bottles in a bag,' he said,
    'so you don't drop them.'
He took the bottles down to the cellar and
    put them on a shelf.
Then he put three of Mrs Mudge's bottles in a bag.

When he came back he was smiling to himself.
He handed the girls a bag with bottles in it.
'I'm afraid you're too late to enter for
    this year's show,' he said, 'but
    I hope your Mum and Dad enjoy the wine.'

Mrs Mudge came into the kitchen.
'Are you girls still here?' she said, crossly.
'We were just going,' said Kate.
'Is your Dad entering his elderberry wine?' asked
    Mrs Mudge. 'It won't beat my dandelion.'

The girls were fed up.
It was too late to enter their dandelion
   wine in the show.
'We'll just have to give it to Mum and Dad,' said Jo.
'All that hard work for nothing!' groaned Kate.

Mum and Dad laughed when Kate told
    them how they made the wine.
'It takes months and months to make
    a good wine,' said Dad.
    'You can't do it in a few days.'

'Never mind,' said Mum. 'I'll open a bottle and
   we'll see what it's like.'
She poured out a glass.
Then she sipped a little of it.
'Good heavens!' she said. 'It tastes delicious!'

Everybody was at the village show.
There were stalls and games and rides and races.
There was a big tent full of flowers and fruit
    and vegetables and cakes and jam and wine.
Everything was ready for the judges.

The judges looked at everything.
They squeezed the vegetables, they felt the fruit
   and they sniffed the flowers.
They tasted the jam and they nibbled the cakes.
They gave prizes for the best.

At last it was time to judge the wine.
The judges had to taste every bottle.
They saved Mrs Mudge's dandelion until last.
Mrs Mudge looked very pleased with herself.
'She's going to win again,' said Dad.

The judges sipped the dandelion wine.
Mrs Mudge smiled.
The judges frowned.
They pulled nasty faces.
The wine was horrible!

Mrs Mudge was furious.

She looked at Mr Mudge.

'I'm sorry, my dear,' he said. 'I must
have muddled up the bottles.'

He gave Kate and Jo a big wink.

'I can't think how it happened!'